Georgia

Rich Smith

Visit us at
www.abdopublishing.com

Published by ABDO Publishing Company, 8000 West 78th Street, Suite 310, Edina, Minnesota 55439 USA. Copyright ©2010 by Abdo Consulting Group, Inc. International copyrights reserved in all countries. No part of this book may be reproduced in any form without written permission from the publisher. The Checkerboard Library™ is a trademark and logo of ABDO Publishing Company.

Printed in the United States.

Editor: John Hamilton
Graphic Design: Sue Hamilton
Cover Illustration: Neil Klinepier
Cover Photo: iStock Photo

Manufactured with paper containing at least 10% post-consumer waste

Interior Photo Credits: AirPhoto/Jim Wark, Alamy, AP Images, Atlanta Braves, Atlanta Falcons, Atlanta Hawks, Atlanta Thrashers, The Coca-Cola Company, Comstock, Corbis, Georgia Dept of Natural Resources, Getty, Granger Collection, Gunter Küchler, iStock Photo, Library of Congress, The Masters Golf Tournament, Michael Fletcher, Mile High Maps, Mountain High Maps, North Wind Picture Archives, One Mile Up, Play Along, Richard Chambers, Robert Bowman, Trail of Tears/Robert Lindneux, US Fish and Wildlife Service/Jane Rohling, and the U.S. Government.

Statistics: State population statistics taken from 2008 U.S. Census Bureau estimates. City and town population statistics taken from July 1, 2007, U.S. Census Bureau estimates. Land and water area statistics taken from 2000 Census, U.S. Census Bureau.

Library of Congress Cataloging-in-Publication Data

Smith, Rich, 1954-
  Georgia / Rich Smith.
     p. cm. -- (The United States)
  Includes index.
  ISBN 978-1-60453-645-4
  1. Georgia--Juvenile literature. I. Title.

F286.3.S64 2010
975.8--dc22
                                2008051032

Table of Contents

The Peach State

Georgia is an Atlantic coastal state in the southeastern United States. Georgia is called the Peach State because the delicious yellow fruit grows especially well in its rich, red soil and warm sunshine.

There is much more to Georgia than peaches. It is a place of great importance to the economy of the United States. Many of the nation's biggest companies are based in Georgia. They have chosen to be there because of Georgia's large and modern cities, good roads and transportation services, and friendly, hard-working people.

Georgia also is a place of beauty. From its coastal lowlands to its majestic mountains are found towering trees, colorful flowers, and adorable animals. There is always something fun to see and do in Georgia.

Sunset over Brickhill River,
Cumberland Island, Georgia.

Quick Facts

Name: Georgia was named in honor of King George II. He was the king of Great Britain from 1727-1760.

State Capital: Atlanta

Date of Statehood: January 2, 1788 (4th state)

Population: 9,685,744 (9th-most populous state)

Area (Total Land and Water): 59,425 square miles (153,910 sq km), 24th-largest state

Largest City: Atlanta, population 519,145

Nickname: The Peach State

Motto: Wisdom, Justice, and Moderation

State Bird: Brown Thrasher

Quartz

State Flower: Cherokee Rose

State Rock: Quartz

State Tree: Live Oak

State Song: "Georgia On My Mind"

Highest Point: Brasstown Bald, 4,784 feet (1,458 m)

Lowest Point: Atlantic Ocean, 0 feet (0 m)

Average July Temperature: 79°F (26°C)

Live Oak

Record High Temperature: 112°F (44°C), in Greenville, August 20, 1983.

Average January Temperature: 47°F (8°C)

Record Low Temperature: -17°F (-27°C), in Floyd County, January 27, 1940.

Average Annual Precipitation: 60 inches (152 cm)

Number of U.S. Senators: 2

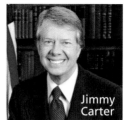
Jimmy Carter

Number of U.S. Representatives: 13

U.S. Presidents Born in Georgia: Jimmy Carter

U.S. Postal Service Abbreviation: GA

Geography

Georgia is in the southern United States. The southeastern corner of Georgia borders the Atlantic Ocean. Georgia's neighbor to the northeast is South Carolina. North Carolina and Tennessee border Georgia in the north. To the west is Alabama. Florida borders southern Georgia.

Georgia is the 24th-largest state. It covers 59,425 square miles (153,910 sq km). Its three main regions include the southern Coastal Plain, the central Piedmont, and the northern mountains.

The Coastal Plain is the largest region. It extends across half the state. It is mostly low and flat. Sea level is its lowest elevation. This point is found where land meets the waters of the Atlantic Ocean.

TENNESSEE

NORTH CAROLINA

SOUTH CAROLINA

Atlanta

Athens

Augusta

ALABAMA

Columbus

Savannah

GEORGIA

N

Chattahoochee River

Chattahoochee River

Altimaha River

Savannah River

Suwannee River

ATLANTIC OCEAN

0   100 miles
0   100 km

FLORIDA

Georgia's total land and water area is 59,425 square miles (153,910 sq km). It is the 24th-largest state. The state capital is Atlanta.

The highest point in Georgia is Brasstown Bald. It is a small peak that rises 4,784 feet (1,458 m) above sea level. It is located in the Blue Ridge Mountains in the

Brasstown Bald is the highest point in Georgia. It is in the steep, rugged Blue Ridge Mountains.

northern part of the state. The other main mountain chain that runs through northern Georgia are the Appalachian Mountains.

The Piedmont is a plateau region. It rises about 2,000 feet (610 m) above sea level in the north. It gradually lowers to about 200 feet (61 m) in the south.

The most important
rivers in Georgia
are the Savannah,
Altamaha, Suwannee,
and Chattahoochee. The
Chattahoochee River is
the longest. The largest
inland body of water
is Lake Lanier. The
Okefenokee Swamp on
the Florida border is all
that remains of an ancient
shallow sea. Along the
coast of Georgia are 13
barrier islands.

The Okefenokee Swamp is all that
remains of an ancient shallow sea.

Climate and Weather

The Coastal Plain and Piedmont regions of Georgia have a subtropical climate. That means the summers are sticky hot and the winters mild.

The northern mountains have a more moderate climate. Summers are warm. Winters are cold and often snowy.

The average July temperature for the entire state is about 79°F (26°C). The average January temperature is 47°F (8°C). The hottest it has ever been in Georgia is 112°F (44°C). That happened on August 20, 1983, in the city of Greenville. The coldest temperature was recorded on January 27, 1940. The temperature that day in Floyd County dropped to -17°F (-27°C).

Georgia is normally a wet state. It receives about 60 inches (152 cm) of rain annually. The wettest part of the state is the Coastal Plain. The Coastal Plain is the area closest to Florida and the Atlantic Ocean.

Small tornadoes are common in Georgia. Hurricanes also sometimes strike the state.

Lightning strikes through the fog in Atlanta, Georgia.

Plants and Animals

The live oak is the official state tree of Georgia. It is called a "live" oak because it does not lose its leaves in

Spanish moss hangs from live oak trees on a path on Georgia's Cumberland Island.

winter. Live oaks in Georgia are most common in the Coastal Plain and on the barrier islands. They grow about 50 feet (15 m) tall, and their wood is very sturdy. Other trees that grow in Georgia include white hickory, maple, pine, red cedar, and sweet gum.

The beautiful Cherokee rose is Georgia's official flower. It has bright white petals and a yellow center. It grows on a shrub that loves to climb. The shrub can grow to a height of 33 feet (10 m).

Many types of wildflowers grow in Georgia. One of them is the azalea.

Cherokee Rose

Azalea

It is the state's official wildflower. Other wildflowers include daffodils, black-eyed Susan, corn poppy, Indian blanket, lemon mint, sunflower, showy primrose, and yellow cosmos.

Many kinds of animals live in Georgia. The white-tailed deer gets its name because the underside of its tail is white. But, mostly the white-tailed deer is red-brown. Its color changes to gray-brown in the fall and winter.

A deer at Georgia's Cumberland Island National Seashore.

Also found in Georgia are black bears, opossums, minks, raccoons, muskrats, skunks, rabbits, flying squirrels, mice, and snakes. The gopher tortoise is the state's official reptile. The green tree frog is its official amphibian. The honeybee is the official insect. The brown thrasher is the official bird. The official fish is the largemouth bass. The official marine mammal is the right whale.

Gopher
Tortoise

Honeybee

Right Whales

Green Tree Frog

History

Among the first people to live in Georgia were Native Americans. They belonged to the Creek and Cherokee Nations. They greeted

A Creek Indian village.

explorers who came from Europe in the 1500s.

No one is sure who was the first European to reach Georgia. Some say it was Juan Ponce de León of Spain. Others say it was Lucas Vasquez de Ayllon in 1526. Ayllon tried to start a colony in the area that year. Many believe the state's first European visitor was actually Spain's Hernando de Soto in 1540.

Spain claimed Georgia until 1733. That was the year James Oglethorpe of England arrived with a group of colonists at what now is the city of Savannah. The Spanish and English fought over control of Georgia for almost 10 years after that. The English won, and the Spanish were driven out.

Native Americans greet James Oglethorpe and the first English settlers in Georgia in 1733.

The British government at first did not allow Georgia's colonists to own slaves. But, that changed in the 1750s. Slaves were brought in to help grow and harvest cotton, rice, sugar cane, and indigo.

Young and old slaves harvest cotton on a Georgia farm.

In 1776, Georgia joined with the 12 other American colonies in their war for independence from Great Britain. The British army

The British army captured Savannah, Georgia, during the Revolutionary War.

captured Savannah in 1778. They controlled most of Georgia until the year before the Revolutionary War officially ended in 1783.

The government of the new United States was created by a document called the Constitution. Georgia was the fourth colony to sign it. Doing so made Georgia officially a state. That happened on January 2, 1788.

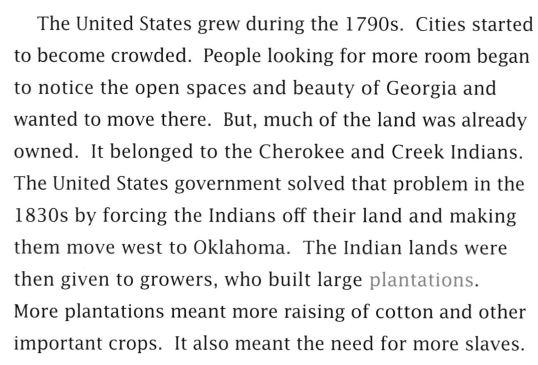

The United States grew during the 1790s. Cities started to become crowded. People looking for more room began to notice the open spaces and beauty of Georgia and wanted to move there. But, much of the land was already owned. It belonged to the Cherokee and Creek Indians. The United States government solved that problem in the 1830s by forcing the Indians off their land and making them move west to Oklahoma. The Indian lands were then given to growers, who built large plantations. More plantations meant more raising of cotton and other important crops. It also meant the need for more slaves.

Slaves became so important in Georgia that the state went to war against the United States government in 1861 rather than let those in bondage go free. This was known as the Civil War. It lasted until 1865, when Georgia and 10 other Southern states were defeated. In the end, the slaves were given their freedom.

The ruins of an Atlanta, Georgia, train station in 1864.

Destroyed homes in Savannah, Georgia, during the Civil War.

Much of Georgia was destroyed after the Civil War. However, civic leaders pushed to rebuild the state as quickly as possible and to industrialize. Industrializing was important because it opened the door to progress. And progress is what has made modern Georgia a happy and prosperous state today.

Did You Know?

- Four other cities besides Atlanta have been the capital of Georgia at different times in the past. They are Savannah, Augusta, Louisville, and Milledgeville.

- Georgia once made it against the law to slap a friend on the back, or on Sundays to carry an ice cream cone in a back pocket. Atlanta made it illegal to tie giraffes to telephone poles.

- Coca-Cola was invented in Georgia. Dr. John Pemberton was a pharmacist from Atlanta. He invented the formula of the famous soft drink in 1886.

- The rain that falls on the south and east sides of Atlanta ends up flowing into the Atlantic Ocean. But the rain that falls on its north and west sides ends up flowing into the Gulf of Mexico.

- Kids all around the world went crazy for Cabbage Patch Kids dolls in the 1980s. The dolls were invented by an art student from the town of Cleveland, Georgia. Cabbage Patch Kids are still sold in toy stores everywhere. But in Cleveland, there is a place called Babyland General Hospital. Hand-sewn original Cabbage Patch dolls are made there.

People

Jimmy Carter (1924-) was the 39th president of the United States. He served as president from 1977 to 1981. He came to Washington, D.C., promising to make the federal government more honest and trusted. Carter was the governor of Georgia before being elected president. Earlier, he was a member of the Georgia Senate. Carter won the Nobel Peace Prize in 2002. He was born in Plains, Georgia.

Jimmy Carter received the Nobel Peace Prize on December 10, 2002. Only two other former presidents (Theodore Roosevelt and Woodrow Wilson) have received this important honor.

Martin Luther King, Jr.
(1929-1968) was a leader in the civil rights movement during the 1950s and 1960s. He was born in Atlanta, Georgia. He believed that Americans should be judged not by the color of their skin but by who they are on the inside. His famous "I Have a Dream" speech in 1963 paved the way for new laws

Dr. Martin Luther King, Jr. waves to the crowd at the Lincoln Memorial for his "I Have a Dream" speech on August 28, 1963.

giving blacks full equality with whites. King received the Nobel Peace Prize in 1964. He was murdered in Memphis, Tennessee, in 1968. King's birthday, January 15, is set aside as a national holiday in his honor.

Ray Charles (1930-2004) was one of the biggest names in music. He played piano and saxophone. He was also a singer who composed many of his own tunes. Charles helped define modern American rhythm-and-blues music. He won 12 Grammy Awards during his career. Charles became blind when he was seven years old. He was born in Albany, Georgia.

Margaret Mitchell (1900-1949) wrote a novel in 1936 that became one of America's favorites. The book was *Gone With the Wind*. It was about life in Georgia around the time of the Civil War. In 1939, it was made into a movie that won 10 Academy Awards. Mitchell was born in Atlanta.

Jackie Robinson (1919-1972) was the first African American person to break the color barrier in Major League Baseball. His being picked to play on the Brooklyn Dodgers in 1947 meant that blacks could no longer be kept off Major League Baseball teams. His baseball career ended in 1956. Before that, he and his team reached the World Series six times. He was born in Cairo, Georgia.

Juliette Gordon Low (1860-1927) started the Girl Scouts of the United States of America in 1912. She believed that such a group was needed to teach young girls about caring and good citizenship, as well as sports and the outdoors. Low was born in Savannah, Georgia.

Cities

Atlanta is Georgia's capital and largest city. Atlanta has a population of 519,145. It is located in the Piedmont region of the state. The city started in 1837 as a railroad depot with only six buildings. At first, the town's name was Terminus. It was then changed to Marthasville. The name became Atlanta in 1847. The city was burned to the ground during the Civil War. Today, Atlanta is one of the most important cities in the United States. Only New York City and Houston, Texas, are home to more of the nation's biggest companies.

Augusta is the second-largest city in Georgia. The city's nickname is the Garden City of the South. Its population is 192,142. The city was founded in 1736. It is named in honor of Great Britain's Princess Augusta (1719-1772). The city is located on the border with South Carolina in the east-central part of Georgia.

Augusta's nickname is the Garden City of the South.

It has a very important medical school, and every year hosts a major golf tournament called The Masters.

Columbus has a population of 187,046. It is the third-largest city in the state. Columbus was founded in 1828 on a bluff above the Chattahoochee River in the west-central part of Georgia. Insurance and high-technology businesses are very important to Columbus's economy. One of the city's youth baseball teams won the Little League World Series in 2006.

Savannah is the fourth-largest city of Georgia. It has a population of 130,331. The city was founded in 1733. It was the capital of Georgia during Colonial times. The city is located on the Savannah River near where the river empties into the Atlantic Ocean. Savannah has a busy seaport. It is also a place that manufactures small jet airplanes, construction equipment, and paper products.

Athens is in the northeast part of Georgia. It is the state's fifth-biggest city. Its population is 112,760. The city's nickname is the Classic City. Athens is home to the University of Georgia. The city is proud of its Pulitzer Prize-winning book authors, annual bicycle races, and music scene.

Transportation

Hartsfield-Jackson Atlanta International Airport is the world's busiest airport. About 90 million passengers come and go through its 196 gates each year. The runways handle almost 1 million takeoffs and landings annually.

A jet takes off while another lands at Hartsfield-Jackson Atlanta International Airport. This is the busiest airport in the world.

Georgia is connected to the farms and factories of the world through the Port of Savannah. Another important Georgia seaport is located in the Atlantic coastal city of Brunswick. Port Bainbridge is an inland port where the Apalachicola, Chattahoochee, and Flint Rivers meet. Also on the Chattahoochee River is Port Columbus.

Much of the freight passing through these ports arrives by train. There are two major freight railroads serving Georgia. Trains just for passenger travel also crisscross the state.

A light rail train crosses the highway near Atlanta, Georgia.

Georgia has nearly 115,000 miles (185,075 km) of public roads. Four major interstate highways carry cars, trucks, and buses through Georgia. They include I-75, I-20, I-85, I-16, and I-95.

Natural Resources

Almost 30 percent of Georgia's 37 million acres (15 million hectares) of land are used for agriculture. The most important farm products are chickens and eggs, cotton, flowers, and beef.

A Georgia chicken farm.

Georgia is the number-one state for peanuts sold to other countries. Georgia farms also are famous for growing tasty peaches. Georgia is nicknamed the Peach State.

The Atlantic Ocean port city of Brunswick was once known as the shrimp capital of the word because its fishermen caught so many of the prized shellfish. Shrimp are still an important catch in Georgia. So are snapper, grouper, and other saltwater fin fish. Georgia's plentiful freshwater fish include trout, catfish, bluegill, perch, bass, and jackfish.

Shrimp

Much lumber is harvested from Georgia's nearly 24 million acres (9.7 million ha) of forests. Most of the lumber comes from pine trees. The remainder comes from hardwood trees.

Nearly one-fourth of the clay produced in the United States is mined in Georgia. Other mineral goods from the state include iron oxide pigments, feldspar, granite, construction stone, and cement.

Industry

The headquarters for Cartoon Network is in Atlanta.

Georgia's most important industries include the making of fabrics and clothing, heavy construction machinery, paper products, lumber, furniture, paints, electrical equipment, bricks and floor tiles, ceramics, glass, aircraft, and automobiles. Georgia also has many companies that provide financial services, or help travelers enjoy their visits to the state.

Many of the largest American companies are based in Georgia.   They include AT&T Mobility, Delta Airlines, UPS, Home Depot, Aflac, Rubbermaid, Primerica Financial Services, SunTrust Banks, and Georgia-Pacific.

Some companies from Georgia are not only big, but are also household names. The Cartoon Network is one of them. Cable News Network, the Weather Channel, Chick-Fil-A, Arby's, and the Waffle House are a few others. Then there is the Coca-Cola Company. It was started in Georgia more than a century ago. It is now the world's largest maker of soft drinks.

Coca-Cola was first sold in a drug store in Atlanta. Today it is the largest maker of soft drinks.

Sports

Georgia has major league teams in baseball, football, basketball, and hockey. All are based in the city of Atlanta.

Baseball's Atlanta Braves moved from Milwaukee, Wisconsin, in 1966. One of the team's most famous players was outfielder Hank Aaron. He hit 755 home runs during his career.

Hank Aaron played for the Braves from 1954-1974.

ATLANTA
FALCONS

The year 1966 also saw the beginnings of the Atlanta Falcons. They are Georgia's National Football League team.

ATLANTA HAWKS

A much older team is the National Basketball Association's Atlanta Hawks. The Hawks started playing in 1949.

The youngest of Georgia's major sports  teams is the Atlanta Thrashers. They play in the National Hockey League. Their first game was in 1999.

 Professional golf is popular in Georgia. A major golf tournament called The Masters is played each year in Augusta.

Another popular sport in Georgia is car racing. The state has more than 20 speedways and drag strips.

Atlanta hosted the Summer Olympic Games in 1996. Athletes have brought gold medals home to Georgia from several earlier Olympic Games.

Georgia has 28 colleges and universities that belong to the National College Athletic Association.

The 1996 Summer Olympics were held in Atlanta.

Entertainment

Atlanta is the heart of Georgia's arts and entertainment world. It is home to an opera company and a symphony orchestra. There also are a number of wonderful museums. These include the Georgia Museum of Art, the Oglethorpe University Museum of Art, the High Museum of Art, and the Morris Museum of Art.

The city of Macon hosts the Georgia Music Hall of Fame. One of the reasons it was put in Macon is that Macon was the birthplace of the kazoo.

A kazoo.

Georgia has more than 50 different library systems. Together their shelves carry about 15 million books, magazines, and other works. Some of those books were written by authors from Georgia. These include Alice Walker, Flannery O'Connor, Carson McCullers, and Margaret Mitchell.

Festivals and fairs are held throughout the year across the state to celebrate the many good things about Georgia.

The Wiener Dog Race is held each year in Savannah, Georgia. Money raised during the event helps a local pet shelter.

Timeline

5000 BC—The first humans arrive in Georgia. They later group into various Native American tribes.

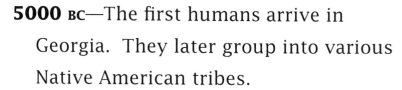

HERNANDO
DE SOTO

1540—Spanish explorer Hernando de Soto travels through Georgia.

1733—Spain's claim to Georgia is challenged by England when James Oglethorpe starts a colony at Savannah.

1776—Georgia joins other colonies fighting for independence from Britain.

1788—Georgia becomes the fourth state admitted to the United States.

1830s—Native Americans are forced to leave Georgia.

1861—Georgia quits the United States in order to keep slavery legal. The American Civil War begins.

1865—Georgia and all other rebel Southern states are defeated. Slaves are freed.

1886—Dr. John Pemberton creates and sells Coca-Cola in Atlanta, Georgia.

1977—Jimmy Carter is sworn in as president of the United States.

2008—Atlanta-based Delta Air Lines merges with Northwest Airlines to become the world's largest airline.

Glossary

Barrier Island—Long and narrow landform just offshore from a mainland. Typically made up of sand, silt, or pebbles.

Civil Rights Movement—A nationwide effort beginning in the 1950s to reform federal and state laws so that blacks could enjoy full equality with whites.

Civil War—The war fought between the Northern and Southern states from 1861-1865. The Southern states were for slavery. They wanted to start their own country. Northern states fought against slavery and a division of the country.

Colony—A place settled by people from someplace else. Usually, the settlers remain under the control of the government of the place from which they came.

Hurricane—A violent windstorm that begins in tropical ocean waters and moves in a generally northerly direction. It begins to break up after it reaches land. But before that, it causes tides to rise dangerously high along shorelines and brings deadly waves, driving rain, and even tornados.

Industrialize—To change a society or location from one in which work is done mainly by hand to one in which work is done mainly by machines.

Piedmont—An Italian word that means "at the foot of the hills."

Plain—A large, flat area of land. There are few trees on plains. Many plains are filled with grasses.

Plantation—A large piece of land in which crops, like cotton, coffee, or tobacco, are raised and harvested by workers who live there.

Plateau—A large area of land that is mainly flat but much higher than the land that neighbors it.

Index